D1222375

Whales

By Valerie J. Weber

Reading Consultant: Susan Nations, M.Ed.,
author/literacy coach/consultant in literacy development

WEEKLY READER®
PUBLISHING

Please visit our web site at www.garethstevens.com.
For a free catalog describing our list of high-quality books,
call 1-800-542-2595 (USA) or 1-800-387-3178 (Canada).
Our fax: 1-877-542-2596

Library of Congress Cataloging-in-Publication Data

Weber, Valerie.
     Whales / by Valerie J. Weber.
         p. cm. — (Animals that live in the ocean)
     Includes bibliographical references and index.
     ISBN-10: 0-8368-9567-3   ISBN-13: 978-0-8368-9567-4 (lib. bdg.)
     ISBN-10: 0-8368-9577-0   ISBN-13: 978-0-8368-9577-3 (softcover)
     1. Whales—Juvenile literature. I. Title.
  QL737.C4W388   2008
  599.5—dc22   2008009598

This edition first published in 2009 by
Weekly Reader® Books
An Imprint of Gareth Stevens Publishing
1 Reader's Digest Road
Pleasantville, NY 10570-7000 USA

Senior Managing Editor: Lisa M. Herrington
Senior Editor: Barbara Bakowski
Creative Director: Lisa Donovan
Designer: Alexandria Davis
Cover Designer: Amelia Favazza, *Studio Montage*
Photo Researcher: Diane Laska-Swanke

Photo Credits: Cover, pp. 7, 9, 11, 15, 17, 19 © SeaPics.com;
p. 1 © Chua Han Hsiung/Shutterstock; p. 5 © Digital Vision;
p. 13 © Doug Perrine/naturepl.com; p. 21 © Sue Flood/naturepl.com

Printed in the United States of America

1 2 3 4 5 6 7 8 9 10 09 08

Table of Contents

Who Is This Giant?. 4

A Breath of Fresh Air 8

Baby Whales and Adult Whales . . 12

Long Trips 20

Glossary. 22

For More Information. 23

Index 24

Boldface words appear in the glossary.

Who Is This Giant?

A huge tail lifts out of the sea. Down comes the tail, slapping the water. What kind of animal has a tail so big?

4

Whales can be very big!
The blue whale is the world's
largest animal. It is as long
as three school buses
in a row!

blue whale

A Breath of Fresh Air

Many other kinds of whales swim in the ocean. Like people, they need to breathe air. They come to the top of the water to breathe.

A whale breathes through its **blowhole**. The animal squirts water and air out of the blowhole. Its spray flies high in the air.

Baby Whales and Adult Whales

A baby whale is called a **calf**. It is born underwater. The mother whale pushes the calf to the surface for its first breath.

calf

A mother whale feeds its calf milk. A whale calf drinks 50 gallons of milk each day. Could you drink that much milk?

Some adult whales eat tiny plants and animals called **plankton** (PLANK-tuhn). A whale gulps huge amounts of water and plankton. The whale lets out the water through its mouth.

mouth

Other whales chase big groups of fish. A whale opens its mouth wide around the fish. Then the whale snaps its mouth shut.

mouth

Long Trips

Many kinds of whales travel far every year. They swim from warm seas to cold seas. There, they find plenty of fish and plankton to eat.

Glossary

blowhole: opening on top of a whale's head through which it breathes air

calf: a baby whale or other animal

plankton: small animals and plants that live in water

For More Information

Books

Amazing Whales! I Can Read! (series).
Sarah L. Thomson (HarperCollins Publishers, 2006)

Killer Whales. Seymour Simon (Seastar Books, 2002)

Whales. Animal Lives (series). (Teacher Created Resources, 2006)

Web Sites

Whale Times: Fishin' for Facts
www.whaletimes.org/whales.htm
Learn about the different parts of whales, what they eat, and more.

Zoom Whales
www.enchantedlearning.com/subjects/whales
Learn all kinds of facts about whales, and print whale outlines to color!

Publisher's note to educators and parents: Our editors have carefully reviewed these web sites to ensure that they are suitable for children. Many web sites change frequently, however, and we cannot guarantee that a site's future contents will continue to meet our high standards of quality and educational value. Be advised that children should be closely supervised whenever they access the Internet.

Index

blowhole 10

blue whale 6

breathing 8, 10, 12

calf 12, 14

fish 18, 20

milk 14

mouth 16

plankton 16, 20

size 6

tail 4

About the Author

A writer and editor for 25 years, Valerie Weber especially loves working in children's publishing. The variety of topics is endless, from weird animals to making movies. It is her privilege to try to engage children in their world through books.